Notice

Mention of specific companies, organizations or authorities in this book does not imply endorsement by the author, publisher, nor does mention of specific companies, organizations or authorities imply that they endorse this book.

© 2009 Nathan Manley

All rights reserved. No part of this publication may be reproduced or transmitted in any form or by any means, electronic or mechanical, including photography, recording or any other information storage and retrieval system, without the express written consent of the author.

The EDGE: A Swimmer's Every Day Guide to Excellence may be purchased by visiting www.livewellswimfast.com

Cover art by Sue Mann (sue@digitalmann.com).

Book Design by Nathan Manley.

Photos by Madonna Fox and Josh Fox.

In memory of Coaches Richard Quick and Jimmy Flowers.

Acknowledgements

First and foremost, I would like to thank Dave Denniston, Dr. Alan Goldberg, Bob Steele and Amanda Drerup who, without hesitation, generously contributed their experience and wisdom to this book. The swimming world is fortunate to have such quality people as yourselves working with and teaching our young people.

To my editors and reviewers: Tim Jasperse, David Kieft, Dad, Sue Mann and others, thank you for your honesty and insight.

A special thank you goes out to all of my swimmers, present and past, for inspiring this project, posing for pictures and being my guinea pigs.

Thank you to my wife, Jodi, who saw the acronym in "edge" and thus created the title of this book. Proof yet again that you make everything I do better. Thank you for supporting this project 100%.

About the Authors

Coach Nathan Manley has been teaching swimmers since 1995. He is an ASCA certified coach and an Order of Ikkos recipient (awarded to coaches of Olympic/Paralympic medalists). Nathan holds a masters degree in physical education with a specialization in coaching from Ball State University.

Dave Denniston was a national champion for Auburn University in 1999 and a member of the 2000 World Championship team in the 200 breaststroke. Dave also made 3 videos with GoSwim on breaststroke technique. In 2005 Dave was paralyzed from the waist down in a sledding accident in Wyoming. After considerable rehabilitation and learning to swim all over again, he earned a spot on the 2008 Beijing Paralympic Team and was appointed captain. Today Dave is a sought after speaker and clinician sharing his experiences and encouraging people to discover and apply a positive attitude to their every day lives.

Amanda Drerup earned a BS in nutrition from Samford University and became a Registered Dietitian through Michigan State University. Her swimming background and coaching experience combined with her expertise in nutrition have made her a valuable consultant to age groupers and international level swimmers alike.

As a sports psychology consultant, Dr. Alan Goldberg works with swimmers at every level from Olympians right down to age groupers. A popular presenter at the Olympic Training Center, swim coaches clinics and clubs around the country, Dr. G specializes in helping individual swimmers get unstuck and swimming fast when it counts the most. He is the author of *Smoke on the Water, DMTS (Developing Mentally Tough Swimmers)* and *Swimming Fast When it Counts the Most*. Dr. G has also produced two CD sets: *Swimming Out of Your Mind* and *The Racer's Edge*. In addition, Dr. G is a regular contributor to Swimming World Magazine.

Bob Steele coached for 46 years at all levels of swimming. He produced championship teams at Peoria Richwoods and Deerfield High Schools in IL, Justus Aquatics in FL, Wichita Swim Club in KS and at Northwestern University, Southern Illinois University, and Cal-State Bakersfield. Coach Steele served as USA Swimming Director of Athlete and Coach Development for 9 years and has lectured on swimming around the world. Currently, he operates Winning Spirit Racing Camps and makes presentations at clinics.

Getting Started Guide

Let's be honest. You are not alone. There are thousands of swimmers out there working hard in the pool every day. Subsequently there are a lot of fast swimmers. If you think you are pretty fast, look up the event rankings on the USA Swimming website. You might be surprised to see just how many fast swimmers there are. Let's say you are a sixteen year old girl, just as an example, and your 100 butterfly time in short course yards is :59.99. That's a pretty good fly time, but did you know over 500 sixteen year olds broke a minute in the 100 butterfly in 2008? So the question is: if there are so many good swimmers out there, how do you set yourself apart? How do you gain an edge on all that competition?

The answer: you have to do more than just swim hard at practice every day.

That's where *The EDGE* comes in. *The EDGE* has been developed by coaches, swimmers and other sports professionals to help you work on all those things which don't fit neatly into a practice like visualization, goal setting, nutrition tracking.

So, whether you are starting a high school season, a summer long course season, a middle school season or a short club season, *The EDGE* will challenge you every day to do more than just work hard, and give you the tools you need to gain an edge on the competition.

Let's give you an overview of the opportunities inside *The EDGE*. Seven categories have been developed, one for each day of the week: **Read, Respond, Record, Rehearse, Research, Reflect** and **Refocus**. The following pages will introduce you to each and how to use them.

Refocus

The first day of each week is the refocus day. The purpose of the refocus day is to keep your goals and your goal achievement strategies in the forefront of your mind. You'll be using the chart you see below. You will fill out the chart every week with the same information until you reach your goal. Then you can start a new goal and continue through the process. You'll receive more instruction on how to use the refocus chart later in this book.

Goal	Visualization details
Strategies	
Check Point	
Achievement details	

Read

Most of *The EDGE* is designed to help you analyze your own swimming experience. The read day, however, gives you a break from writing and an opportunity to learn about technique (with Dave Denniston), character (with Coach Nathan Manley) and the components of success (with Coach Bob Steele).

Respond

The respond days have been developed by sports psychologist, Dr. Alan Goldberg. As Dr. Goldberg points out, "Races are won and lost before the start and finish because of the interrelationship between your mind, body and performance."

Dr. Goldberg's exercises will help you see exactly how your thoughts impact your performances.

Rehearse

On the rehearse days, Coach Bob Steele will help you learn to use visualization as a means to prepare mentally for races to come.

Record

The record days will allow you to track your recovery habits. Each of the squares you see in the chart below next to sleep is equal to one hour. You will check off a box for each hour of sleep you had since practice the day before. Similarly, each square in the rows of the food groups represent one serving. You'll check a square for each serving you consume that day. Lastly, you will record your resting heart rate. This is best done when you first wake up in the morning. Take your pulse for 60 seconds and record the number. Always start your pulse counting with zero.

The Record day moves around each week so you are not always evaluating the same day of the week and even though you'll only be recording your habits once per week, you should be able to recognize any issues you might be having. Pay attention to how your training goes on the days you record. If you have a tough day, it may likely be related to poor hydration, too few calories or not enough sleep.

Each record day also includes some advice from registered dietician, Amanda Drerup. Athletes have different nutritional needs than the average sedentary individual. Between your own records and some insight from Amanda, you'll be able to fuel your body and help it recover so you can train and race well.

Hours of sleep								
Glasses of Water								
Grains								
Fruits/Veggies								
Milk Products								
Protein								
Resting Heart Rate								

Research

In today's world, so much information is available on the internet. The research days will help you build a list of links where you can find some great information, pictures, videos, stories, interviews and more.

Reflect

At the end of each week, you will find the reflect day. This day gives you the opportunity to review your training and racing for the week and a place to record all the positives which occurred. People in general find it much easier to recall and to focus on the negatives, but negative thoughts lead to negative actions. By consistently tracking the positives, you'll have a log of the good work you've been doing to encourage you.

Why Write?

Some of you may find the writing exercises in this book challenging, but writing is important. Everyone dreams about swimming fast. That's easy. If you want to be really good, though, you have to take your dreams and turn them into written goals, strategies and reflections so that instead of daydreaming all the time, you actually live the dream.

The format of *The EDGE* and even the various sections were designed to force you to write. *The EDGE* will be a record of your experience. Your hand will write out your goals every week, record the steps and missteps and ultimately pen your story. You are not just learning from someone else's experience, you are learning from your own! No two copies of *The EDGE* will ever be the same even if you complete one every year.

IMPORTANT NOTICE TO SWIMMERS:

You should make your coach aware that you are using *The EDGE* to supplement your training. If you encounter any conflict between what your coach tells you and what you read in *The EDGE*, talk to your coach about it.

<u>Your coach is the final authority on all things swimming because your coach knows you best.</u>

Just a few tips before you begin:

- Start your work in *The EDGE* on Monday so that at the very beginning of every week, you start with your goal setting page.

- Keep your copy of *The EDGE* in a place where you will SEE it every day, such as in your swim bag or on your night stand. If you hide it on a shelf, you'll forget to work in it. Keep it visible.

- Work in *The EDGE* every day. There might be days you like less than others, but they all work together, so stay with it. (It is *The Swimmer's **Every Day** Guide to Excellence*!)

- We recommend you work in *The EDGE* just before you go to bed. If that doesn't work for you, pick another consistent time and place.

- Give an honest effort. Five minutes a day is not a significant sacrifice to move closer to your goals. Don't treat it like homework that just has to get done. Consider *The EDGE* your swimming diary.

- Flip back through the book, especially when you're tired or down. Previous successes will pick you up and re-energize you for the next day.

Now, grab a pen or pencil. Your *EDGE* experience begins on page 16.

Refocus

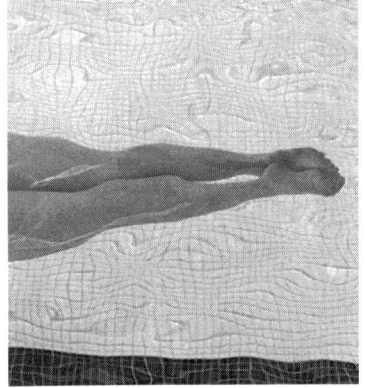

> Champions are champions not because they do anything extraordinary but because they do the ordinary things better than anyone else.
>
> -Chuck Noll

| Week 1 | Monday | Tuesday | Wednesday | Thursday | Friday | Saturday | Sunday |

Before you start filling out your weekly goal page, let's review the key components of good goal setting.

Goal: Your goal should be a number so you can easily determine the moment of achievement. Let's use breaking a minute in the 100 yard freestyle as an example. Your goal is :59.99.

Visualization details: Decide when and where you want to achieve your goal. Not only will your deadline motivate you, but you can also use the time and place in your visualization drills.

Strategies: Don't hope you'll meet your goal, determine how to meet it. What is the weakest part of your 100 free? If it's the start, spend 5 minutes a week with your coach after practice on your start. You might select a practice attendance goal or try to increase the number of your underwater dolphin kicks. Two or three measureable strategies is plenty.

Check Point: Give yourself a small goal on the way to your end of season goal. There might be a test set at practice or pre-taper race time you would like to meet. Your goal could be to complete a set of 50s on long rest under :30 or break 1:02.00 in the 100 before taper.

Achievement Details: When you meet your goal, write it down. Write the time, date and place and any personal comments you like.

Week 1   Monday   Tuesday   Wednesday   Thursday   Friday   Saturday   Sunday

The Streamline Habit

Chances are that you already know the technique points we're going to cover in this short season edition of *The EDGE*, but the question is, "Do you actually practice them?" Our goal is to make the basic, essential techniques in swimming AUTOMATIC. We are going to cover four areas absolutely essential to swimming races successfully. We will cover one every three weeks. At the beginning of the three weeks, I'll give you some tips and throughout the three weeks, there will be pictures to remind you what habit we're working on.

Our first task is to make good streamlining a habit. Streamlining is not only the easiest way to go through the water, but it is also *faster than swimming*.

The basics of proper streamline go like this: 1) stack your hands one on top of the other and squeeze, 2) squeeze your upper arms against the sides of your head, 3) keep your back straight by pulling your belly button in toward your spine and 4) squeeze your legs together and point your toes. If you streamline properly, you should be able to get your whole body past the flags before you need to kick.

-Send it Forward, Dave

Read

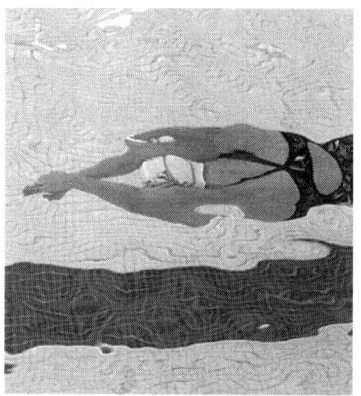

I know of no more encouraging fact than the unquestionable ability of man to elevate his life by conscious endeavor.

-Henry David Thoreau

Rehearse

> Enthusiasm is one of the most powerful engines of success...Nothing great was ever achieved without enthusiasm.
>
> -Ralph Waldo Emerson

Week 1   Monday   Tuesday   **Wednesday**   Thursday   Friday   Saturday   Sunday

Introduction to Visualization

Since we're using visualization as part of our goal achievement strategy, let's make sure we know how to do it well. Over the next few weeks, you will be practicing some visualization techniques with Coach Steele. Visualization is when you imagine swimming the perfect race. It takes practice to get good at visualization, so even if you can't see anything at first, that's o.k. Just think your way through it until you get better at creating images. Here are some tips to keep in mind as you practice.

1. Always start your visualization with a few minutes of relaxation.

2. Visualize in as much detail as possible, using all of your senses.

3. Keep your visualization to about 10 minutes including relaxation.

4. Imagine what you want to happen, not what you are afraid will happen. If your visualization turns negative at any point, stop and play the scene back until you get what you want.

From *Swimming Fast When it Counts the Most*, Dr. Alan Goldberg

| Week 1 | Monday | Tuesday | Wednesday | Thursday | Friday | Saturday | Sunday |

Enter your current best times in the chart below.

Event	Flat Start Time	Relay Split
50 freestyle		
100 freestyle		
200 freestyle		
400/500 freestyle		
800/1000 freestyle		
1500/1650 freestyle		
50 butterfly		
100 butterfly		
200 butterfly		
50 backstroke		
100 backstroke		
200 backstroke		
50 breaststroke		
100 breaststroke		
200 breaststroke		
200 IM		
400 IM		

Respond

Good is the enemy of great.

-Jim Collins

Research

> All the resources we need are in the mind.
>
> -Theodore Roosevelt

Week 1   Monday   Tuesday   Wednesday   Thursday   **Friday**   Saturday   Sunday

Finding Technique Help On-Line

Visit http://www.goswim.tv

You can search any of the technique habits discussed in this book and see great still pictures and videos there. Be sure to bookmark any pages you find especially useful.

Net Notes:

_____

_____

_____

_____

_____

_____

_____

_____

Week 1	Monday	Tuesday	Wednesday	Thursday	Friday	Saturday	Sunday
Hours of sleep (including naps)							
Glasses of Water (8oz = glass)							
Grains (cup pasta, cereal)							
Fruits/Veggies (apple, salad, juice)							
Milk Products (yogurt, cheese)							
Protein (piece of fish, egg)							
Resting Heart Rate (take upon waking)							

See page 11 for a refresher on the Record Day.

Record

Food Facts: Hydration

If your practice is 90 minutes or longer, you should be drinking a sports drink to help replace fluids, electrolytes and calories. If your practice is shorter than an hour and a half, just drinking water is ok.

-Amanda Drerup, RD

You need to play with supreme confidence, or else you'll lose again, and then losing becomes a habit.

-Joe Paterno

Reflect

Most battles are won before they are fought.

-Sun Tzu

| Week 1 | Monday | Tuesday | Wednesday | Thursday | Friday | Saturday | Sunday |

List training sets you performed especially well on this week:

List the timed swims (practice or competition) from this week of which you're proud:

What technical improvement did you make this week:

Any other victories?

Week 2 Monday Tuesday Wednesday Thursday Friday Saturday Sunday

Goal	Visualization details

Strategies

Check Point

Achievement details

See pages 9 and 16 for a refresher on the Refocus page.

Refocus

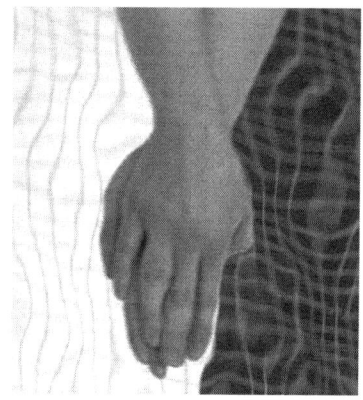

The ascent of Everest was not the work of one day...It is, in fact, a tale of sustained and tenacious endeavor by many over a long period of time.

-Sir John Hunt

Read

> The achiever is the only individual who is truly alive. I see no difference between a chair and the man who sits in the chair, unless he is accomplishing something.
>
> -George Allen

Week 2 Monday **Tuesday** Wednesday Thursday Friday Saturday Sunday

What's 3 seconds?

I hope you're tackling those technique habits every day. Swimming fast has so much to do with the little things you are working on with Dave. In fact, a few years ago, USA Swimming compiled the following research that highlights the importance of how the little things can help a swimmer. They tested many performance characteristics of an Olympian, who swam 25.4 in the 50 meter freestyle, and another swimmer who swam 28.4 in the 50 meter freestyle. After analyzing all the facts and figures, they determined the differences between the two swimmers were:

1) The Olympian went 1 yard further on her start than the other swimmer

2) The Olympian's turnover was .02 faster per stroke than the other swimmer

3) The Olympian pushed back 2 inches further on each arm stroke

Those were the only objective differences between an Olympian and a state level competitor. Think about that the next time your hit the pool.

Week 2	Monday	Tuesday	Wednesday	Thursday	Friday	Saturday	Sunday
Hours of sleep (including naps)							
Glasses of Water (8oz = glass)							
Grains (cup pasta, cereal)							
Fruits/Veggies (apple, salad, juice)							
Milk Products (yogurt, cheese)							
Protein (piece of fish, egg)							
Resting Heart Rate (take upon waking)							

See page 11 for a refresher on the Record Day.

Record

Food Facts: Hydration

Are you drinking between 8-12 cups (64-96 oz) of fluid daily?
The best way to check your hydration level is to check your urine. If your urine is bright yellow and stinks, you need to drink more water.

-Amanda Drerup, RD

When I played with Michael Jordan on the Olympic team...what impressed me most was that he was always the first one on the floor and the last one to leave.

-Steve Alford

Rehearse

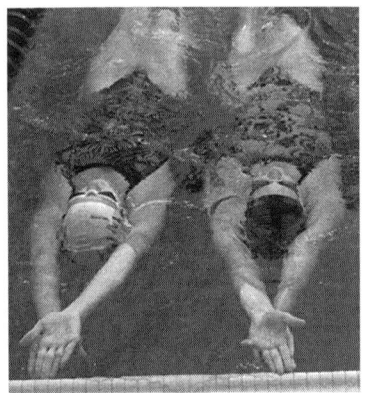

For every failure, there's an alternative course of action. You just have to find it. When you come to a roadblock, take a detour.

-Mary Kay Ash

Week 2   Monday   Tuesday   Wednesday   **Thursday**   Friday   Saturday   Sunday

Starting Visualization with Relaxation

Developing the ability to relax is an important part of visualization. Here's a 5 minute relaxation program you can practice.

1. Lie or sit down in a quiet place and close your eyes.

2. Start by focusing on your breathing. Breath in for a 5 count, hold the breath for 5, exhale for 5 and count 5 before inhaling again. Repeat pattern for 1 minute or 3 cycles.

3. Next focus on relaxing some of the major muscle groups. Shrug your shoulders up to your ears and then relax. Squeeze your shoulder blades together and relax. Flex each arm by clenching your fist and tensing all your arm muscles and then relax. Repeat with your upper legs; flex and relax. Repeat if necessary.

4. Finish by picturing yourself in a relaxing scene. It might be the beach, a field of grass, a hammock or even your bed. Go back to your controlled breathing. Each time you exhale, feel yourself sink a little farther into the sand or grass or mattress.

Be the best you can be—Coach Steele

Week 2 Monday Tuesday Wednesday Thursday **Friday** Saturday Sunday

Nutrition Help Online

Visit http://www.usaswimming.org. Click on the "swimmers" tab and then click on the "swimmers resources" link in the menu on the left hand side. There you will find the "nutrition tracker." You'll need a USA Swimming account to access the nutrition tracker, but you should have one anyway so you can take full advantage of the tools on the USA Swimming site. The tracker will be a great supplement to Amanda's tips on nutrition.

Net Notes:

_____

_____

_____

_____

_____

Research

You don't have to let yourself be terrorized by other people's expectations of you.

-Sue Patton Thoele

Respond

> Develop a love for details. They usually accompany success.
>
> -John Wooden

Week 2 Monday Tuesday Wednesday Thursday Friday **Saturday** Sunday

Does what I think really matter?

Races are won and lost before the start and finish because what you think or say to yourself both before and during your swims goes instantly and directly into your body and touches off some subtle physiological changes. These small physical changes, in turn, significantly affect how fast you swim. Review the chart below. Put an 'X' in the box next to the descriptions you have experienced.

Physical Reactions to Negatives	Impact on Performance	X
Muscles tighten	Stroke shortens, rhythm is disrupted, reaction time increases, discomfort, fatigue and oxygen debt intensify	
Breathing gets faster and shallower	Muscles tighten, even more and interfere with normal breathing patterns, kills endurance	
Digestion shuts down	Feelings of nausea set in	
Hands and fees get cold as blood flow is directed away from the extremities.	Feel for the water is impaired	

From *Swimming Fast When it Counts the Most*, Dr. Alan Goldberg

| Week 2 | Monday | Tuesday | Wednesday | Thursday | Friday | Saturday | Sunday |

List training sets you performed especially well on this week:

Reflect

List the timed swims (practice or competition) from this week of which you're proud:

What technical improvement did you make this week:

Any other victories?

They can conquer who
believe they can.

-Virgil

Refocus

> Character—the willingness to accept responsibility for one's own life—is the source from which self respect springs.
>
> -Joan Didion

Week 3	Monday	Tuesday	Wednesday	Thursday	Friday	Saturday	Sunday

Goal	Visualization details

Strategies

Check Point

Achievement details

See pages 9 and 16 for a refresher on the Refocus page.

Week 3   Monday   Tuesday   Wednesday   Thursday   Friday   Saturday   Sunday

The Components of Success

You can boil success in any sport down to three components:

Skill: In swimming skill refers to your stroke technique, starts, turns, finishes, breakouts, underwater work, etc.

Fitness: How in shape you are

Motivation: Specifically, your ability to motivate yourself to train, to work on skills and to get up and race

To be really successful, you have to have a high level of skill, fitness and motivation. Rank yourself in the three components above. Put a 3 next to the area you think is your best. Put a 1 next to the component you need to work on the most and put a 2 next to the remaining component. Then turn your weakness into a strength.

_____ Skill   _____ Fitness   _____ Motivation

Be the Best You Can Be, Coach Steele

Read

The person who makes a success of living is the one who sees his goal steadily and aims for it unswervingly. That is dedication.

-Cecil B. DeMille

Respond

> Insanity is doing the same thing over and over and expecting a different result.
>
> -Albert Einstein

Week 3   Monday   Tuesday   **Wednesday**   Thursday   Friday   Saturday   Sunday

In order for you to learn to swim fast when it counts the most you must first develop awareness of what you are currently doing mentally that may very well be slowing you down. Sit down, close your eyes and mentally review, in as much detail as possible, a previous <u>bad</u> swim. What were your self talk and thoughts…

Day of the race?

During the race?

During warm up?

If and when things went bad?

Just before the race?

In the final length?

On the blocks and at the start?

Right at the finish?

From *Swimming Fast When it Counts the Most*, Dr. Alan Goldberg

Week 3	Monday	Tuesday	Wednesday	Thursday	Friday	Saturday	Sunday
Hours of sleep (including naps)							
Glasses of Water (8oz = glass)							
Grains (cup pasta, cereal)							
Fruits/Veggies (apple, salad, juice)							
Milk Products (yogurt, cheese)							
Protein (piece of fish, egg)							
Resting Heart Rate (take upon waking)							

See page 11 for a refresher on the Record Day.

Record

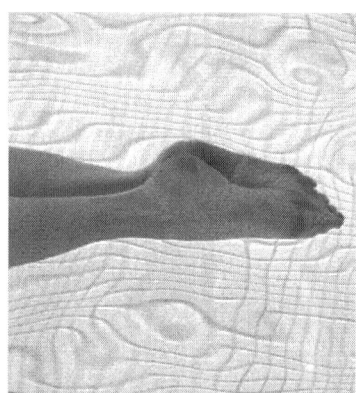

Your subconscious mind does not argue with you. It accepts what your conscious mind decrees. If you say, ["I can"], your subconscious mind works to make it true.

-Dr. Joseph Murphy

Food Facts: hydration

If you drink too much prior to racing or working out hard, you'll probably overload your stomach. Try this strategy: 2—3 hours before swimming, consume about 16 ounces of water or sports drink. Then drink about 8 ounces more 15 minutes or so before warm up.

-Amanda Drerup, RD

Rehearse

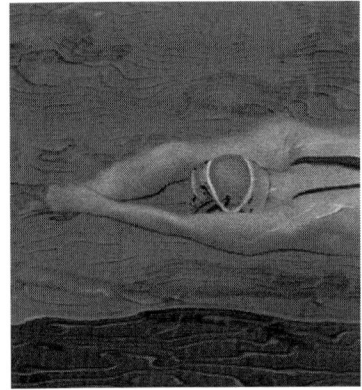

Make the present good and
the past will take care of itself.

-Knute Rockne

Week 3 Monday Tuesday Wednesday Thursday **Friday** Saturday Sunday

Visualization: Setting the Scene

A few days ago, you learned a relaxation exercise to help you get ready for visualization. After performing your relaxation routine, it's time to move your mind to the pool. The more of your senses you can engage the better. Depending on the type of visualization you are doing, you want to picture either a pool from a past swim or a pool where you'll swim in the future. Go through each of the five senses and take a few seconds to try to use them to set the scene for your visualization.

See: the pool, balcony, water, lane lines, teammates, scoreboard, starting blocks (can you see in color too?)

Hear: coaches, teammates, spectators, officials

Feel; the air, water, temperatures

Smell: air, chlorine,

Taste: water

Be the best you can be—Coach Steele

Week 3   Monday   Tuesday   Wednesday   Thursday   Friday   **Saturday**   Sunday

Your coach is the best and most readily available resource you have. Over the past three weeks you have been focusing on making streamline a habit. Find time today before or after practice or even during a set to have your coach evaluate your streamline and give you some feedback. If you get some feedback, jot it down below for future reference.

_____

_____

_____

_____

_____

_____

_____

Research

A successful person realizes his personal responsibility for self-motivation. He starts with himself because he possesses the key to his own ignition switch.

-Kemmons Wilson

Reflect

Week 3   Monday   Tuesday   Wednesday   Thursday   Friday   Saturday   Sunday

List training sets you performed especially well on this week:

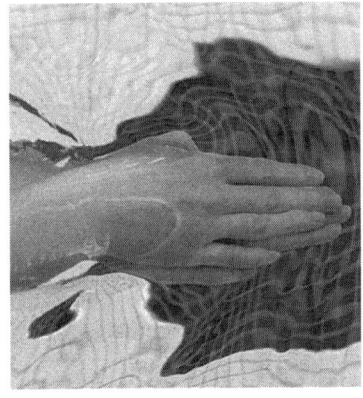

List the timed swims (practice or competition) from this week of which you're proud:

What technical improvement did you make this week:

Any other victories?

> The heights by great men reached and kept were not attained by sudden flight, but they while their companions slept, were toiling upward in the night.
>
> -Henry Wadsworth Longfellow

Week 4   Monday   Tuesday   Wednesday   Thursday   Friday   Saturday   Sunday

Goal	Visualization details
Strategies	
Check Point	
Achievement details	

Refocus

Take calculated risks. That is quite different from being rash.

-George S. Patton

See pages 9 and 16 for a refresher on the Refocus page.

Read

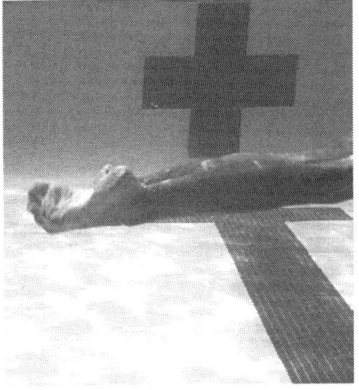

Worry a little bit every day and in a lifetime you will lose a couple of years. If something is wrong, fix it if you can, but train yourself not to worry. Worry never fixes anything.

-Mary Hemingway

Week 4   Monday   Tuesday   Wednesday   Thursday   Friday   Saturday   Sunday

Underwater dolphin kick—Make it a Habit

These days, if you're not good at underwater kicking, you're not going to win. With a good upper body streamline position and a strong kick, you can cover ground as fast or faster than you can swim at the surface.

Get comfortable kicking on all four sides. The dolphin kick is an effective weapon on your back, stomach and side. Many swimmers actually find they are better underwater dolphin kickers when they are toward their side. Kicking in both directions is essential to developing a good underwater kick too. Think of making your body move like a fish does– streamlined front, fin kicking both directions.

To practice, find a landmark about 5—7 meters away from the wall. (go high-tech with a streamline noodle from www.gamesgimmickschallenges.com). Try to dolphin kick to that spot EVERY time you leave the wall. When you get comfortable doing that well, pick a new land mark farther out and get comfortable underwater dolphin kicking to that spot. If you want to watch someone do it well, Natalie Coughlin (world record holder 100 meter backstroke) is a great underwater kicker.

Send it Forward—Dave

Week 4   Monday   Tuesday   **Wednesday**   Thursday   Friday   Saturday   Sunday

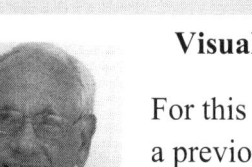

Visualization Exercises: Lifetime Best

For this exercise, we're going to go back in time to a previous lifetime best swim. Go through the relaxation routine you've practiced and then set the scene for the pool at which you swam the lifetime best you want to visualize. Next...

See yourself get up on the blocks. Hear the starter's whistles, the "take your mark" command and the beep! Watch yourself swim your lifetime best with the strokes, strategy, pace and feelings you had during that race and see yourself celebrate at the end of the race.

Reviewing a past race is a great way to practice your visualization skills for future races.

Try this exercise at least once a day for the next week. It can be the same race every time if you like or you may recall different lifetime best races.

Be the best you can be—Coach Steele

Rehearse

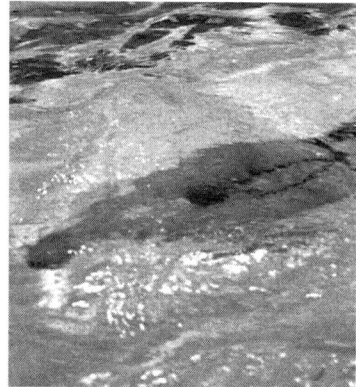

If you are going to be a champion, you must be willing to pay a greater price than your opponent.

-Bud Wilkinson

Research

> I learned the only way you are going to get anywhere in life is to work hard at it. If you do, you'll win. If you don't, you won't.
>
> -Bruce Jenner

Week 4   Monday   Tuesday   Wednesday   **Thursday**   Friday   Saturday   Sunday

Sports Psychology Help Online

Visit Dr. Goldberg's website at www.competitivedge.com. You can sign up for Dr. Goldberg's email newsletter. Write your username and password below and any other interesting things you notice as you browse through the site.

Net Notes:

_____

_____

_____

_____

_____

_____

_____

_____

Week 4	Monday	Tuesday	Wednesday	Thursday	Friday	Saturday	Sunday
Hours of sleep (including naps)							
Glasses of Water (8oz = glass)							
Grains (cup pasta, cereal)							
Fruits/Veggies (apple, salad, juice)							
Milk Products (yogurt, cheese)							
Protein (piece of fish, egg)							
Resting Heart Rate (take upon waking)							

See page 11 for a refresher on the Record Day.

Record

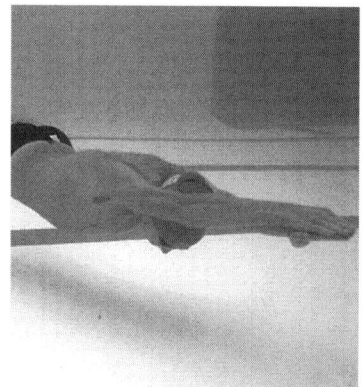

When you're interested in doing something, you do it when it's convenient. When you're committed to something, you accept no excuses, only results.

- Ken Blanchard

Food Facts: Post Meet/Practice Eating

Try to eat a meal as soon as you can after a workout or meet. Doing so will help to replace the muscle energy you used up swimming and aid in recovery for the next workout or competition day. Carbohydrate loading isn't necessary; just eat a well-balanced meal.

-Amanda Drerup, RD

Respond

Week 4   Saturday

Last week you reviewed your self talk and thoughts before and during a bad race. Now let's pick a race where you were extremely satisfied with how fast you swam. Review the performance in your mind as vividly as possible. What were you thinking...

Day of the race?

During the race?

During warm up?

If and when things went bad?

Just before the race?

In the final length?

Wisdom comes from an equal balance of experience and reflection.

-Aristotle

On the blocks and at the start?

Right at the finish?

From *Swimming Fast When it Counts the Most*, Dr. Alan Goldberg

| Week 4 | Monday | Tuesday | Wednesday | Thursday | Friday | Saturday | Sunday |

List training sets you performed especially well on this week:

Reflect

List the timed swims (practice or competition) from this week of which you're proud:

What technical improvement did you make this week:

> Success is about having, excellence is about being. Success is about having money and fame, but excellence is being the best you can be.
>
> -Mike Ditka

Any other victories?

Refocus

If a man loves the labor of his trade, apart from any question of success of fame, the gods have called him.

-Robert Louis Stevenson

| Week 5 | Monday | Tuesday | Wednesday | Thursday | Friday | Saturday | Sunday |

Goal	Visualization details
Strategies	
Check Point	
Achievement details	

See pages 9 and 16 for a refresher on the Refocus page.

Week 5   Monday   Tuesday   Wednesday   Thursday   Friday   Saturday   Sunday

The Fourth Component

Earlier in this book my friend and colleague, Coach Bob Steele, astutely identified three components of success: skill, fitness and motivation. It is a tried and tested formula. Yet I find there are swimmers who possess adequate skill, fitness and motivation, but never seem to reach their full potential.

Let me be clear: success in the pool does in fact require efficient technique, properly developed aerobic and anaerobic capacities and a serious internal drive. There is nothing out there which will allow an athlete to bypass these requirements. However, there is a fourth component which needs our attention.

The Fourth Component is character. Character is a set of traits so ingrained in us that we are hardly aware of its influence though it guides everything we do and say. To change or mold these traits requires a commitment to extensive daily practice and habit making. It is not a genetic blessing or stroke of luck. Mastering and applying The Fourth Component is the result of a clear choice which anyone can make.

Live Well. Swim Fast.—Coach Manley

Read

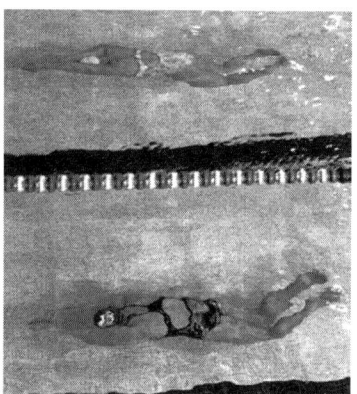

Most people give up just when they're about to achieve success. They quit on the one-yard line.

-H. Ross Perot

Rehearse

> Don't believe everything you hear—even in your own mind.
>
> -Daniel G. Amen M.D.

Week 5 Monday Tuesday **Wednesday** Thursday Friday Saturday Sunday

Visualization Exercises: Flawless Fifty

Go through the relaxation routine you've practiced and then set the scene for your home competition pool (if you don't have a home competition pool, set the scene for a familiar pool). We're going to visualize a flawless fifty meter swim. Select 10 aspects you will focus on like the list below. Be sure to include a few of the things you have been working on with your coach. When you get good at meters, try a 50 short course and add a perfect turn to your list. Practice this once a day for the next week.

1. Quick start
2. Streamline entry
3. Powerful underwater kicks/pullout
4. Perfectly timed breakout
5. Powerful kicks
6. Long, powerful strokes
7. Breath control
8. Touching the pad
9. Seeing a best time
10. Celebrating

Be the best you can be—Coach Steele

Week 5   Monday   Tuesday   Wednesday   **Thursday**   Friday   Saturday   Sunday

Interviews and Insight Online

Visit www.swimnetwork.com and www.floswimming.com

There you will find great racing to analyze and interviews of top level swimmers and coaches.

Net Notes:

_____

_____

_____

_____

_____

_____

_____

Research

The successful man has enthusiasm. Good work is never done in cold blood; heat is needed to forge anything.

-Harry Truman

Week 5   Monday   Tuesday   Wednesday   Thursday   **Friday**   Saturday   Sunday

Respond

Let's compare the bad and good swims you wrote about in the past two weeks. On the left, make a list of the things you concentrated on before and during your bad swim. On the right, list what you focused on before and during your good swim.

Bad Swim	Good Swim

Now that you are viewing them side by side, hopefully you can see some patterns in your concentration. You want to avoid spending time thinking about and concentrating on the "bad" list. Become familiar with the "good" list as those areas of concentration have produced good swims in the past. When you recognize yourself focusing on things from the "bad" list, switch over to a "good" list item.

From *Swimming Fast When it Counts the Most*, Dr. Alan Goldberg

> Four things cannot come back: the spoken word, the spent arrow, the past life an a neglected opportunity.
>
> -Arabian Proverb

Week 5	Monday	Tuesday	Wednesday	Thursday	Friday	Saturday	Sunday
Hours of sleep (including naps)							
Glasses of Water (8oz = glass)							
Grains (cup pasta, cereal)							
Fruits/Veggies (apple, salad, juice)							
Milk Products (yogurt, cheese)							
Protein (piece of fish, egg)							
Resting Heart Rate (take upon waking)							

See page 11 for a refresher on the Record Day.

Record

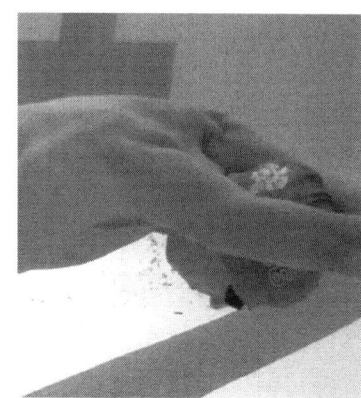

Things turn out the best for those who make the best of the way things turn out.

-Art Linkletter

Food Facts: Grains

Common examples of grains include bread, pasta, cereal and tortillas. In fact the grain group is typically the easiest food group to consume since any food made of wheat, cornmeal, barley, oats, cereal grains or rice is considered a grain. You may need to eat between 10 and 12 ounces each day.

-Amanda Drerup, RD

Reflect

> Success is a matter of understanding and religiously practicing specific, simple habits that always lead to success.
>
> -Robert J. Ringer

Week 5 | Monday | Tuesday | Wednesday | Thursday | Friday | Saturday | Sunday

List training sets you performed especially well on this week:

List the timed swims (practice or competition) from this week of which you're proud:

What technical improvement did you make this week:

Any other victories?

| Week 6 | Monday | Tuesday | Wednesday | Thursday | Friday | Saturday | Sunday |

Goal	Visualization details

Strategies

Check Point

Achievement details

See pages 9 and 16 for a refresher on the Refocus page.

Refocus

History has demonstrated that the most notable winners usually encountered heartbreaking obstacles before they triumphed. They won because they refused to become discouraged.

-B.C. Forbes

Read

> You are today where your thoughts have brought you; you will be tomorrow where your thoughts take you.
>
> -James Allen

Week 6 Monday Tuesday Wednesday Thursday Friday Saturday Sunday

Character Trait #1: Enthusiasm

Enthusiasm and excitement are not the same. People get excited about things which are going to happen to them. Enthusiasm, on the other hand, is an internal choice that has real lasting power. People are enthusiastic about the things they are going to do. Consider these basic tenets:

- **Practice enthusiasm:** how often do you drag in to practice wishing you were somewhere else? Approach your training with enthusiasm and you'll get a lot more out of every session.

- **Act as if:** Everyone has days when they find it difficult to be enthusiastic. The key is to act as if you are enthusiastic. Before you know it, you'll become enthusiastic.

- **The extra push:** Enthusiasm will not keep you from encountering obstacles, but it will be the reason you stick with it.

- **Filling the enthusiasm tank:** the best way to keep yourself enthusiastic is to be enthusiastic about what others are doing.

Be Enthusiastic. Swim Fast.—Coach Manley

Week 6	Monday	Tuesday	Wednesday	Thursday	Friday	Saturday	Sunday
Hours of sleep (including naps)							
Glasses of Water (8oz = glass)							
Grains (cup pasta, cereal)							
Fruits/Veggies (apple, salad, juice)							
Milk Products (yogurt, cheese)							
Protein (piece of fish, egg)							
Resting Heart Rate (take upon waking)							

See page 11 for a refresher on the Record Day.

Food Facts: Fruit

Athletes in training should consume between 2 and 4 cups of fruit per day. Consume a variety of fruits so you take advantage of all the vitamins and minerals fruits have to offer. Frozen fruit, canned fruit, fruit juice and dried fruit are all healthy choices.

-Amanda Drerup, R.D.

Record

Our envy of others devours us most of all.

-Alexander Solzhenitzyn

Rehearse

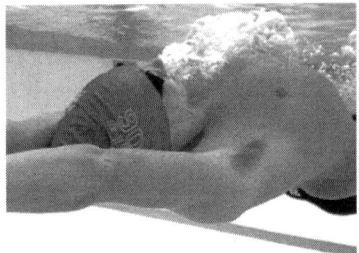

> Decide what you want, decide what you are willing to exchange for it. Establish your priorities and go to work.
>
> -H.L. Hunt

Week 6   Monday   Tuesday   Wednesday   **Thursday**   Friday   Saturday   Sunday

Visualization Exercises: Back-Up Fifties

After going through your relaxation routine, set the scene for the pool where you practice. Perform five flawless 50s. If you make a mistake in any way, see or feel something wrong you must back up and start over again. Repeat this exercise until you perform a flawless 50 (start, breakout, strokes, turns, finishes, strategy, celebration—just like the flawless 50s on page 46).

Complete one flawless 50 at least once a day for the next week.

Be the best you can be—Coach Steele

Week 6   Monday   Tuesday   Wednesday   Thursday   **Friday**   Saturday   Sunday

It's time to tap that greatest of all resources again...you remember, your coach. For the last three weeks you have been concentrating on the skill that has made Olympic Champions like Michael Phelps and Natalie Coughlin the best in the world. Take some time today to see if your coach can evaluate your underwater dolphin kick. If he/she has some suggestions, write them down below so you can refer to them later.

_____

_____

_____

_____

_____

_____

_____

Research

The greatest revolution of our generation is the discovery that human beings, by changing the inner attitudes of their minds, can change the outer aspects of their lives.

-William James

Respond

> Morale is the state of mind. It is steadfastness and courage and hope.
>
> -General George Marshall

Week 6   Saturday

Are You a Practice Swimmer?

Do you swim faster in practice than competition? If you are like a lot of swimmers, then you'd answer a resounding and frustrating "YES". "Why?!" It's likely the answer to these questions is connected to your concentration.

When you go to practice, what do you focus on?

...before you get in the pool? _____

...during warm-up? _____

...just before the race/fast set? _____

...when you begin to get tired? _____

...when people pass you? _____

...going in and out of turns? _____

...in terms of times? _____

...in terms of your competition/teammates? _____

From *Swimming Fast When it Counts the Most*, Dr. Alan Goldberg

Week 6 Monday Tuesday Wednesday Thursday Friday Saturday Sunday

List training sets you performed especially well on this week:

List the timed swims (practice or competition) from this week of which you're proud:

What technical improvement did you make this week:

Any other victories?

Reflect

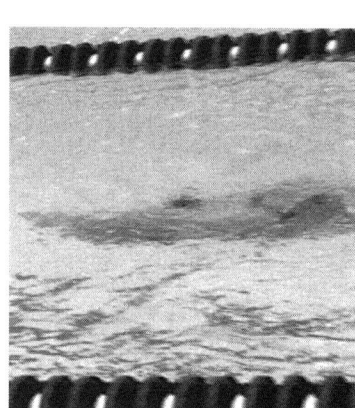

> If you want to achieve a high goal, you're going to have to take some chances.
>
> -Alberto Salazar

Refocus

Every negative event contains within it the seed of an equal or greater benefit.

-Napoleon Hill

Week 7	Monday	Tuesday	Wednesday	Thursday	Friday	Saturday	Sunday

Goal	Visualization details

Strategies

Check Point

Achievement details

See pages 9 and 16 for a refresher on the Refocus page.

Week 7   Monday   Tuesday   Wednesday   Thursday   Friday   Saturday   Sunday

Legal Turns—Make it a Habit

When I was in college at Auburn, we had a rule that if you weren't going to do a perfect fly or breast turn, you had to do a flip turn. The point was that we shouldn't practice bad turns. Neither should you. You certainly don't want to get disqualified because you practice illegal turns, but you'll never be as fast as you can be if you don't execute your races with perfect turns. Eliminate these major errors from your training.

- One hand touches on fly and breast/rolling over too soon on backstroke—I know you get tired at practice and it's "easier" to throw an illegal turn, but you'll get tired in your race too. Defeat that tendency now and when your opponents struggle, you'll thrive.

- Breathing in and out of turns— Spend your time developing skills that are fast. If you break out of your turns to get a breath, then you're not breaking out to race. Teach yourself to hold your breath for the first stroke off the wall for every stroke. Yes, even backstroke and breaststroke.

                              Send it Forward– Dave

Read

When I was young, I never wanted to leave the court until I got things exactly correct. My dream was to become a pro.

-Larry Bird

Rehearse

The individual who is mistake-free is also probably sitting around doing nothing. And that is a very big mistake.

-John Wooden

Week 7   Monday   Tuesday   **Wednesday**   Thursday   Friday   Saturday   Sunday

Visualization Exercises: Goal Time Fifties

Go through the relaxation routine you've practiced and then set the scene for your home competition pool (if you don't have a home competition pool, set the scene for a familiar pool).

You're going to swim a flawless fifty or pace fifty for longer events. Find a stop watch or a clock with a second hand. Sit or lie down so you can't see the clock. Have someone tell you when to start your fifty or just hit the stopwatch button with your finger. Complete your fifty with a signal to your partner like raising a finger or your hand or by just hitting the stop button on your stopwatch. Remember to see yourself celebrate after the race just like you will when you meet your goal.

With some practice, you can make your visualization match your exact goal or pace time making your visualization exercises even more effective. Typically, after three tries, you can get pretty accurate, so stay with it. Complete the goal time visualization exercise every day for the next week.

Be the best you can be—Coach Steele

Week 7   Monday   Tuesday   Wednesday   **Thursday**   Friday   Saturday   Sunday

World Wide Web Gems

Visit www.usaswimming.org. USA Swimming has a 'Tip of the Week' which can usually be found on the home page and under the "swimmers" tab. There is an archive of all the past 'Tips of the Week' you can review too.

Net Notes:

_____

_____

_____

_____

_____

_____

_____

Research

If you sacrifice early, you'll win late.

-Charles Haley

Week 7   Monday   Tuesday   Wednesday   Thursday   **Friday**   Saturday   Sunday

Respond

Sooner or later, those who win are those who think they can.

-Richard Bach

Are You a Practice Swimmer?

When you go to a meet, what do you focus on?

...before you get in the pool? _____

...during warm-up? _____

...just before the race/fast set?_____

...when you begin to get tired?_____

...when people pass you? _____

...going in and out of turns? _____

...in terms of times? _____

...in terms of your competition/teammates? _____

From *Swimming Fast When it Counts the Most*, Dr. Alan Goldberg

Week 7	Monday	Tuesday	Wednesday	Thursday	Friday	Saturday	Sunday
Hours of sleep (including naps)							
Glasses of Water (8oz = glass)							
Grains (cup pasta, cereal)							
Fruits/Veggies (apple, salad, juice)							
Milk Products (yogurt, cheese)							
Protein (piece of fish, egg)							
Resting Heart Rate (take upon waking)							

See page 11 for a refresher on the Record Day.

Food Facts: Vegetables

As an athlete, you probably need to consume 2—4 servings of vegetables daily. Experiment with different ways of preparing and serving vegetables like adding vegetables to a pizza, dipping fresh vegetables in a favorite dip, or adding a small salad to meals.

-Amanda Drerup, R.D.

Record

To be prepared is half the victory.

-Miguel Cervantes

Reflect

| Week 7 | Monday | Tuesday | Wednesday | Thursday | Friday | Saturday | Sunday |

List training sets you performed especially well on this week:

List the timed swims (practice or competition) from this week of which you're proud:

What technical improvement did you make this week:

Be a tough-minded optimist.

-Frosty Westering

Any other victories?

Week 8   Monday   Tuesday   Wednesday   Thursday   Friday   Saturday   Sunday

Goal	Visualization details
Strategies	
Check Point	
Achievement details	

Refocus

> You live up— or down— to your expectations.
>
> -Lou Holtz

See pages 9 and 16 for a refresher on the Refocus page.

Read

The difference between success and failure is doing a thing nearly right and doing it exactly right.

-Edward C. Simmons

Week 8   Monday   Tuesday   Wednesday   Thursday   Friday   Saturday   Sunday

Character Trait #2: Proactive

People who are proactive take control of a situation by making something happen rather than waiting for something to happen. Great athletes are all proactive. Try this:

- **Do for you:** an old Yiddish proverb says, "If you ever need a helping hand, you'll find one at the end of your arm." Stop waiting for someone else to pull, push or drag you up the ladder of success. Climb!

- **Ignore limits:** some never start because they are not sure they can finish. Don't limit yourself to what seems possible or reasonable. Everything seems impossible until you do it. It's ok to dream about winning state, making Olympic Trials or even setting a world record.

- **Make decisions right:** most people spend too much time trying to figure out what the right decision is and end up doing nothing. Don't allow the fear of making a mistake keep you from being proactive. Proactive people make mistakes from time to time, but to do nothing is always a mistake.

Be Proactive. Swim Fast.—Coach Manley

Week 8	Monday	Tuesday	Wednesday	Thursday	Friday	Saturday	Sunday
Hours of sleep (including naps)							
Glasses of Water (8oz = glass)							
Grains (cup pasta, cereal)							
Fruits/Veggies (apple, salad, juice)							
Milk Products (yogurt, cheese)							
Protein (piece of fish, egg)							
Resting Heart Rate (take upon waking)							

See page 11 for a refresher on the Record Day.

Record

Food Facts: Protein

Muscle breaks down during training. Protein is what helps repair muscles. Athletes should consume 6—7 oz per day. In addition to meats and beans, eggs, fish, nuts, seeds, and peas are also an excellent source of protein so pack them full in your diet.

-Amanda Drerup, R.D.

I never blame failures—there are too many complicated situations in life, but I am absolutely merciless toward lack of effort.

-F. Scott Fitzgerald

Rehearse

> It's not the will to win that matters—everyone has that. It's the will to prepare to win that matters.
>
> -Paul "Bear" Bryant

Week 8   Monday   Tuesday   Wednesday   **Thursday**   Friday   Saturday   Sunday

Visualization Exercises: Pre-Race Visualization

Some swimmers find it effective to use visualization just before a race. Some swimmers don't because it increases their anxiety. You'll have to try it and see what works best for you.

For pre-race visualization, we'll use an abbreviated version of your relaxation technique. Just do one cycle of the breathing exercise you learned earlier: Breath in for a 5 count, hold the breath for 5, exhale for 5 and say to yourself, "I am relaxed."

Visualize the important and sometimes faulty parts of your race being done flawlessly. Select things like streamline entry, bounce off walls, finger tip finish, or similar components.

Work with it until you can whittle the whole exercise down to ten to fifteen seconds. Then start practicing the pre-race visualization exercise at practice before timed swims. The next step would be to try it before races at some lesser meets so you can perfect its use before using it before a big swim.

Once perfected you'll have a quick review of the proper techniques necessary for success.

Be the best you can be—Coach Steele

Week 8   Monday   Tuesday   Wednesday   Thursday   **Friday**   Saturday   Sunday

Swimmingworldmagazine.com

Visit www.swimmingworldmagazine.com. If you don't have a subscription to *Swimming World Magazine*, get one. They also have a great technique library. Look for the "Technique" tab in the horizontal menu.

Net Notes:

_____

_____

_____

_____

_____

_____

_____

Research

None of us can change our yesterdays, but all of us can change our tomorrows.

-Colin Powell

Respond

| Week 8 | Monday | Tuesday | Wednesday | Thursday | Friday | Saturday | Sunday |

Are You a Practice Swimmer?

Let's compare what you concentrate on at practices versus meets. Write down the things you listed the last two weeks in your review of your concentration.

| What do you concentrate on at practice? | What do you concentrate on at meets? |

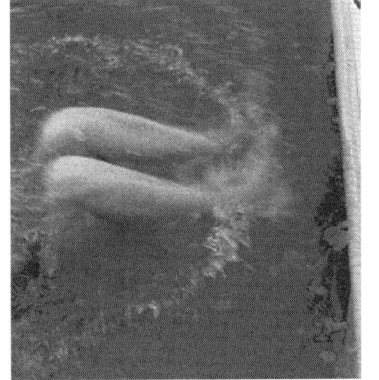

> One of life's most painful moments comes when we must admit that we didn't do our homework, that we are not prepared.
>
> -Merlin Olsen

There is no mystery why many swimmers go faster in practice than at meets. It is directly related to having a different focus of concentration when you swim well as opposed to when you struggle. The first step in developing the concentration of a winner is to become aware of these differences.

From *Swimming Fast When it Counts the Most*, Dr. Alan Goldberg

Week 8 — Monday Tuesday Wednesday Thursday Friday Saturday **Sunday**

List training sets you performed especially well on this week:

Reflect

List the timed swims (practice or competition) from this week of which you're proud:

What technical improvement did you make this week:

> The quality of a person's life is in direct proportion to his commitment to excellence, regardless of his chosen field of endeavor.
>
> -Vince Lombardi

Any other victories?

Refocus

You can't make a great play unless you do it first in practice.

-Chuck Noll

Week 9	Monday	Tuesday	Wednesday	Thursday	Friday	Saturday	Sunday

Goal	Visualization details

Strategies

Check Point

Achievement details

See pages 9 and 16 for a refresher on the Refocus page.

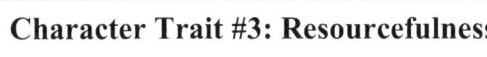

Week 9   Monday   Tuesday   Wednesday   Thursday   Friday   Saturday   Sunday

Character Trait #3: Resourcefulness

Successful people are resourceful. They not only take advantage of all the resources around them, they often glean significant knowledge and experience from sources other people overlook.

How many of the following resources do you access: your coach, the internet, instructional videos, video analysis, books, magazines, older swimmers on your team, competitors, nutritionists, sports psychologists, masseuses, chiropractors, personal trainers, swim camps?

Here are some rules to live by:

- **Talk to Everyone:** "I have never met a man so ignorant that I couldn't learn something from him." - Galileo

- **Watch and Learn:** "You can observe a lot just by watching." - Yogi Berra

- **Read, Read, Read:** "I am a part of all I have read." - John Kieran

Be Resourceful. Swim Fast.—Coach Manley

Read

Out of clutter, find simplicity. From discord, find harmony. In the middle of difficulty, lies opportunity.

-Albert Einstein

Respond

> If you really want something and really work hard and take advantage of opportunities and never give up, you will find a way.
>
> -Jane Goodall

Week 9   Monday   Tuesday   **Wednesday**   Thursday   Friday   Saturday   Sunday

Do you swim better in your "off events" than in your best events?

Do you swim faster in your off events than your best ones? If you are like a lot of swimmers, then you'd answer a resounding and frustrating "YES". "Why?!" It's likely the answer to these questions is connected to your concentration.

When you swim off events, what do you focus on?

...before you get in the pool? _____

...during warm-up? _____

...just before the race/fast set? _____

...when you begin to get tired? _____

...when people pass you? _____

...going in and out of turns? _____

...in terms of times? _____

...in terms of your competition/teammates? _____

From *Swimming Fast When it Counts the Most*, Dr. Alan Goldberg

Week 9	Monday	Tuesday	Wednesday	Thursday	Friday	Saturday	Sunday
Hours of sleep (including naps)							
Glasses of Water (8oz = glass)							
Grains (cup pasta, cereal)							
Fruits/Veggies (apple, salad, juice)							
Milk Products (yogurt, cheese)							
Protein (piece of fish, egg)							
Resting Heart Rate (take upon waking)							

See page 11 for a refresher on the Record Day.

Food Facts: Dairy

Athletes should consume 3—4 cups of dairy products daily.
If drinking milk is not appealing, try incorporating yogurt and cheese into meals to maximize intake of the milk group. Since the meat and fats/oils food groups provide adequate fat, aim for low-fat or fat free milk products.

-Amanda Drerup, R.D.

Record

You must push yourself mentally and physically. A lot of people say John Havlecek never gets tired. Well, I get tired, it's just a matter of pushing myself.

-John Havlicek

Rehearse

> Because a thing seems difficult for you, do not think it is impossible for anyone to accomplish. But whatever is possible for another, believe that you too are capable of it.
>
> -Marcus Aurelius Antoninus

Week 9   Monday   Tuesday   Wednesday   Thursday   **Friday**   Saturday   Sunday

Pre-Race Visualization

Write down the pre-race visualization routine you created last week. Go step by step through what you want to do just before you race.

_____

_____

_____

_____

_____

_____

For the remainder of *The EDGE*, you'll be completing the goal time visualization exercise you practiced on page 60. Just before you visualize stepping up on the blocks, go through your pre-race visualization routine so that you rehearse the entire process of preparing behind the blocks, racing flawlessly and celebrating.

-Be the Best You Can Be, Coach Steele

| Week 9 | Saturday |

Most races are won or lost at the walls. Turn skills are essential to successful swimming. Over the past few weeks you have attempted to make a habit of performing legal, efficient turns. Take some time today to talk to one of your coaches about your turns. See if they can evaluate your turns during a set or after practice. If you get some advice, write it below. If your coach has time, see if he/she can time you flag to flag as you do your turns.

_____

_____

_____

_____

_____

_____

_____

Research

Believe and act as if it were impossible to fail.

-Charles F. Kettering

Reflect

> Imagination is everything. It is the preview of life's coming attractions.
>
> -Albert Einstein

| Week 9 | Monday | Tuesday | Wednesday | Thursday | Friday | Saturday | Sunday |

List training sets you performed especially well on this week:

List the timed swims (practice or competition) from this week of which you're proud:

What technical improvement did you make this week:

Any other victories?

| Week 10 | Monday | Tuesday | Wednesday | Thursday | Friday | Saturday | Sunday |

Goal	Visualization details

Strategies

Check Point

Achievement details

Refocus

You have to believe in yourself when no one else does. That's what makes you a winner.

-Venus Williams

See pages 9 and 16 for a refresher on the Refocus page.

Read

Repeated actions are stored as habits.

-Chuck Knox

Week 10   Monday   **Tuesday**   Wednesday   Thursday   Friday   Saturday   Sunday

Finishes—Make it a Habit

Doing legal finishes should go without saying, but if you're in the habit of touching the wall with one hand in breast or fly or rolling over on your stomach during backstroke swims, it's time to break that habit. Make good, legal finishes your focus for the next four weeks.

Get in the habit of touching underwater with your finger tips. That's where the pad will be; not up in the gutter. Touching with finger tips takes practice. If you don't do it all the time, you're liable to jam your fingers when you try it in a race.

You probably think of streamlining off the wall, but you should also streamline into your finish. Keep your head in line with your spine. If you want to watch someone streamline well on their backstroke finish, find some races with Aaron Piersol. He has a great streamline backstroke finish.

Again it's all about creating habits which transfer into your race. Every time you finish, finish like a race.

Send it forward—Dave

Week 10   Monday   Tuesday   **Wednesday**   Thursday   Friday   Saturday   Sunday

Visualization Takes Practice

Visualizing effectively takes practice. Take time today to perform the goal time visualization exercise from page 60. Be sure to use your pre-race visualization routine as well. The better you get at visualizing the flawless race you want to swim, the more of a positive impact your visualization will have on your actual race.

Rehearse

Learn to do things right and then do them right every time.

-Bob Knight

Research

Diligence is the mother of good luck.

-American Proverb

Week 10   Monday   Tuesday   Wednesday   **Thursday**   Friday   Saturday   Sunday

YouTube? You bet!

Visit www.youtube.com and search "Natalie Coughlin." You'll find several interesting videos. You could do similar searches for your favorite elite swimmers.

Net Notes:

_____
_____
_____
_____
_____
_____
_____
_____

Week 10	Monday	Tuesday	Wednesday	Thursday	Friday	Saturday	Sunday
Hours of sleep (including naps)							
Glasses of Water (8oz = glass)							
Grains (cup pasta, cereal)							
Fruits/Veggies (apple, salad, juice)							
Milk Products (yogurt, cheese)							
Protein (piece of fish, egg)							
Resting Heart Rate (take upon waking)							

See page 11 for a refresher on the Record Day.

Record

Food Facts: Dairy

The milk group provides one the most important minerals in the body, calcium. Calcium is the most abundant mineral in the body and is found in bones, teeth, blood and muscles. Athletes should take a multivitamin if it is difficult to consume the RDA of dairy.

-Amanda Drerup, R.D.

Doubt whom you will, but never yourself.

-Christine Bovee

Respond

Life is full of obstacle illusions.

-Grand Frazier

| Week 10 | Monday | Tuesday | Wednesday | Thursday | Friday | Saturday | Sunday |

Do you swim better in your "off events" than in your best events?

When you swim your best events, what do you focus on?

...before you get in the pool? _____

...during warm-up? _____

...just before the race/fast set? _____

...when you begin to get tired? _____

...when people pass you? _____

...going in and out of turns? _____

...in terms of times? _____

...in terms of your competition/teammates? _____

From *Swimming Fast When it Counts the Most*, Dr. Alan Goldberg

Week 10   Monday   Tuesday   Wednesday   Thursday   Friday   Saturday   Sunday

List training sets you performed especially well on this week:

Reflect

List the timed swims (practice or competition) from this week of which you're proud:

What technical improvement did you make this week:

Never grow a wishbone where your backbone ought to be.

-Clementine Paddleford

Any other victories?

Refocus

Men acquire a particular quality by constantly acting a particular way...you become just by performing just actions, temperate by performing temperate actions, brave by performing brave actions.

-Aristotle

Week 11 Monday	Tuesday Wednesday Thursday Friday Saturday Sunday	
Goal	Visualization details
Strategies	
Check Point	
Achievement details	

See pages 9 and 16 for a refresher on the Refocus page.

Week 11   Monday   Tuesday   Wednesday   Thursday   Friday   Saturday   Sunday

Character Trait #4: Persistence

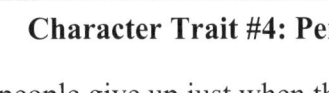

"Most people give up just when they're about to achieve success. They quit on the one-yard line." - H. Ross Perot

You have probably heard the statistics on how many times Abraham Lincoln lost an election before he finally won or how many years Thomas Edison spent trying to perfect the light bulb. Olympic medalist Josh Davis set an American record in the 200 meter freestyle in 1993. Despite his best efforts, he was unable to surpass that time for seven years. Finally at the Sydney Olympics in 2000, he did.

I have worked with lots of swimmers who allow themselves to get frustrated because they haven't improved their time in their favorite event in almost a month. Don't expect to reach your goals without having to exercise some persistence. The question isn't whether you'll experience disappointments, set backs, injuries, illnesses, and an assortment of other potential deterrents during your career. The question is will you be persistent enough, long enough to achieve your goal in spite of them.

Be Persistent. Swim Fast.—Coach Manley

Read

Reflect on your present blessings, of which every man has many; not on your past misfortune, of which all men have some.

-Charles Dickens

Rehearse

> The happiness of your life depends upon the quality of your thoughts.
>
> -Marcus Aurelius Antoninus

Week 11 — Wednesday

Visualization Takes Practice

Have you ever had an incredibly vivid dream and then wondered the next morning whether it really happened or if it was just s dream? Your brain reacts much the same way to effective visualization—it's almost like it really happened. Perform the goal time visualization exercise (from page 60) again today. Use all of your senses to make the vision as real as possible for your mind.

Week 11   Thursday

What's Next?

Have you considered the prospect of swimming in college? Visit www.collegeswimming.com. There you can read up on the latest in NCAA swimming news from all three divisions, see race times and start to get a feel for what might be out there for you.

Net Notes:

_____

_____

_____

_____

_____

_____

_____

Research

The bravest thing you can do when you are not brace is to profess courage and act accordingly.

-Corra Harris

Record

Week 11	Monday	Tuesday	Wednesday	Thursday	Friday	Saturday	Sunday
Hours of sleep (including naps)							
Glasses of Water (8oz = glass)							
Grains (cup pasta, cereal)							
Fruits/Veggies (apple, salad, juice)							
Milk Products (yogurt, cheese)							
Protein (piece of fish, egg)							
Resting Heart Rate (take upon waking)							

See page 11 for a refresher on the Record Day.

When real people fall down in life, the get right back up and keep on walking.

-Michael Patrick King

Food Facts: Fats/Oils

Fat plays several important roles in our body. It is used for energy, helps comprise cell membranes, protect organs, and fat is also necessary to break down vitamins A, D, E, and K which are known as fat-soluble vitamins. Consume fat in moderation and try to eat mostly monounsaturated, but don't eliminate fat from your diet.

-Amanda Drerup, R.D.

Week 11   Monday   Tuesday   Wednesday   Thursday   Friday   **Saturday**   Sunday

Do you swim better in your "off events" than in your best events?

Let's compare what you concentrate on for "off events" versus your best ones. Write down the things you listed the last two weeks in your review of your concentration.

What do you concentrate on for "off events"?	What do you concentrate on for your best events?

Respond

There is no mystery why many swimmers go faster in "off events" than in their best ones. It is directly related to having a different focus of concentration when you swim well as opposed to when you struggle. The first step in developing the concentration of a winner is to become aware of these differences.

From *Swimming Fast When it Counts the Most*, Dr. Alan Goldberg

It's kind of fun to do the impossible.

-Walt Disney

Reflect

| Week 11 | Monday | Tuesday | Wednesday | Thursday | Friday | Saturday | Sunday |

List training sets you performed especially well on this week:

List the timed swims (practice or competition) from this week of which you're proud:

What technical improvement did you make this week:

A bad habit never disappears miraculously; it's an undo-it-yourself project.

-Abigail Van Buren

Any other victories?

| Week 12 | Monday | Tuesday | Wednesday | Thursday | Friday | Saturday | Sunday |

Goal	Visualization details
Strategies	
Check Point	
Achievement details	

See pages 9 and 16 for a refresher on the Refocus page.

Refocus

Having once decided to achieve a certain task, achieve it at all costs of tedium and distaste. The gain in self-confidence of having accomplished a tiresome labor is immense.

-Arnold Bennett

Read

Courage is fear holding on a minute longer.

-General George S. Patton

Week 12   Monday   **Tuesday**   Wednesday   Thursday   Friday   Saturday   Sunday

Character Trait #5: Courage

If you're like most people, you have experienced fear: fear of failure, fear of success, fear of what people will think or say. Fear would extinguish all enthusiasm, paralyze and derail each and everyone of us if we didn't have the ability to be courageous. Courage is not lack of fear, it is what moves us forward in spite of fear.

The ability to be courageous has to be developed and that development starts in practice. Your coach challenges you on a regular basis. There may be intervals, distances or sets which are daunting. Conquer them anyway. Continue to develop your courage at some of the less significant meets in your season. Swim events that scare you. Race competitors who scare you. Ask to anchor a relay if that scares you. Every time you stare down fear will prepare you for that ultimate end of season challenge.

When you warm up for a race, step on the blocks or push off for the final length and feel that sense of fear start to tighten your muscles and cloud your mind, draw on your experiences and exercise your ability to be courageous.

Be Courageous. Swim Fast.—Coach Manley

Week 12	Monday	Tuesday	Wednesday	Thursday	Friday	Saturday	Sunday
Hours of sleep (including naps)							
Glasses of Water (8oz = glass)							
Grains (cup pasta, cereal)							
Fruits/Veggies (apple, salad, juice)							
Milk Products (yogurt, cheese)							
Protein (piece of fish, egg)							
Resting Heart Rate (take upon waking)							

See page 11 for a refresher on the Record Day.

Record

Food Facts: Vitamins and Minerals

Eating a well balanced diet will insure you get the vitamins and minerals you need, but it's ok to take a supplement too. Athletes really need iron, zinc, calcium and vitamin D so make sure any multi-vitamin you take has these key components.

-Amanda Drerup, R.D.

> Our problems are man-made, therefore they may be solved by man. No problem of human destiny is beyond human beings.
>
> -John F. Kennedy

Rehearse

> It's wonderful what we can do if we're always doing.
>
> -George Washington

Week 12   Monday   Tuesday   Wednesday   **Thursday**   Friday   Saturday   Sunday

Visualization Takes Practice

Perfect practice makes perfect. Are you incorporating all the components we've reviewed in your visualization practice?

Relax with a :20 breath or two.

Set the scene incorporating all of your senses.

Perform pre-race visualization just as you will at the actual race.

Perform a flawless goal time race.
(remember to start over if you make an error)

Celebrate!

Week 12   Monday   Tuesday   Wednesday   Thursday   **Friday**   Saturday   Sunday

Talk to your coach about your finishes. As you approach your last meet or two, the competition will get tighter and the difference between 1st and 2nd or sometimes 1st and 8th can be a matter of a good finish. Make sure you are confident about how you are going to perform the last five yards of your races.

Research

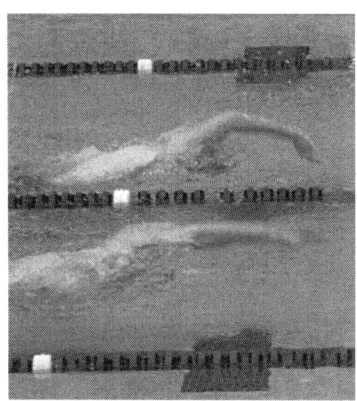

It's really easy to complain. If you're not careful, then you end up complaining about your whole life.

-Lisa Williams

Respond

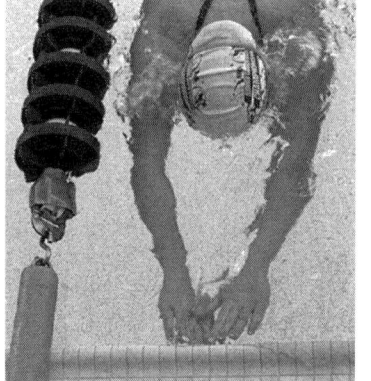

The only limit to our realization of tomorrow will be our doubts of today.

-Franklin D. Roosevelt

Week 12   Monday   Tuesday   Wednesday   Thursday   Friday   Saturday   Sunday

Enter your current best times in the chart below then determine your improvement when compared to your times on page 17.

Event	Flat Start Time	Improve	Relay Split	Improve
50 freestyle				
100 freestyle				
200 freestyle				
400/500 freestyle				
800/1000 freestyle				
1500/1650 freestyle				
50 butterfly				
100 butterfly				
200 butterfly				
50 backstroke				
100 backstroke				
200 backstroke				
50 breaststroke				
100 breaststroke				
200 breaststroke				
200 IM				
400 IM				

Week 12   Monday   Tuesday   Wednesday   Thursday   Friday   Saturday   Sunday

What was the most challenging practice or set you completed this season?

Reflect

What race time are you most proud of from this season? Why?

What would you say was the most significant technical change/ improvement you made this season?

The sign of intelligent people is their ability to control emotions by the application of reason.

-Marya Mannes

Parting thoughts...

We hope you had a great season and if *The Swimmer's EDGE* contributed to your success in any way, we're pleased. You're not done with *The EDGE* yet though. This book ought to become a part of your resource library. Not only can you go back through it to refresh your memory about all the ways you can improve in the pool, but you will also have a whole season of your own comments about training and racing. Just flipping through the pages may be enough to get you enthusiastic about the next season or for your off-season training. You will have documentation of how you took responsibility for your success and made it happen. Your notes will remind you, too, of the ups and downs, thrills and defeats and highlight the power of persistence in any endeavor. And in future seasons, when things don't go your way, pull out this copy of *The EDGE* and encourage yourself with your past successes.

If you enjoyed *The EDGE*, you might also like the long season edition—32 weeks of insights, exercises and quotes to keep you out in front of the competition. For a copy of *The EDGE* or related products, visit www.livewellswimfast.com.

Printed in Great Britain
by Amazon.co.uk, Ltd.,
Marston Gate.